Through It All, Praise!

Praise!

by Dr. Araia Hadgu

Date: 2013

"Poems"

Bless the Lord, O my soul:
and all that is within me, bless his holy name!
Bless the Lord, O my soul,
and forget not all his benefits: (Psalms 103:1-2)

Table of Contents

Introduction

*T*hree decades have passed since I started composing some of these poems in the early 1980's. As an immigrant, full time college student, working full time and raising children was not easy, but had interest in writing. Most of these poems center about life's experiences. Some may sound to be fiction, but are nevertheless real. Throughout the years, I have been inspired by events to be able to add more poems. Especially, having grand-children was an impetus to compose more. In moments of reminiscence, I returned to edit the poems.

The poems consist of biblical truths, anniversaries, congratulations, true stories, fiction, challenges, and advices. They were written at different times and different experiences. I hope and believe these poems will inspire readers to share their ideas with others. I was encouraged by the way friends responded when they read some of these poems. If nothing, our grand children will treasure them when they get to be old enough to read them.

The tile of the book "*Through It All*" summarizes how God has brought us through many difficulties to a land of freedom and safety. It is my hope and prayer that these poems will bless readers. To God be the glory.

Acknowledgement

$\mathcal{M}$y parents died at an early age survived by five children and an infant. Two of my sisters and I were taken in to an orphanage of Evangelistic Faith Missions in what is now Eritrea, East Africa. Later on my brother joined us. If it were not for the missionaries and those that supported the orphanage we grew up in, no telling what our destination would have been. I have the deepest appreciation for those who made it possible for me and my siblings to get educated and live a better life. I owe a debt I cannot repay no matter what I do and however hard I try. I believe God will reward them from his riches in glory through Christ whom they served all their life time. Of those missionaries, some have gone to be with the Lord and some are still alive and of age.

Poem one:

Ayn`Alem

Houses like these

Are homes of his

That lives in place

So close in space

Neighbors in love

A gift from above.

These are houses but only a few
Representation of typical view.
You see homes in rows
Of dirt roofs nothing aglow.

In one houses of this size
May live as many as nine.
There is no quarrel or repine
No problem, everything is fine.

A small candle of light
Dispels darkness at night.
Usually there is a coal of fire
A flickering flame aid the sight.

At meal all wait for the father to pray
And give thanks for another safe day.
Each receives a portion, it's the way,
And dip in spicy soup in a pan of clay.

Members sit about and share and laugh.

Many times there may not be enough,

But share what they have no matter tough

To keep everyone go on however rough.

But many face death and grope

Beg for food but not even a drop.

With no one around to help them cope

To eternity they slip without any hope.

Who would claim a crown of life and solace

In heaven, God's abode a wonderful place,

Except he that is born of God through grace,

By faith on Christ & his death for Adam's race?

A young boy lived among them

Whose name was Ayn`Alem.

A symbolic name it was an omen,

A leading man to be among men.

Life for him was only scourging poverty,

From infancy he knew nothing but scarcity.

As nature refused to bring forth its bounty,

Lack became the norm of his community.

In time he grew bony hunger stricken

Yearned for food but nothing was given.

With harsh winter wind his body beaten

Nothing but helplessness in him was seen.

In a very chilly and cold day .....

He found a place to crawl and lay

In a barn where calves rest and play.

He covered himself under the hay,

"This is warm, warm," he did say.

In a moment he was half asleep,

Saw a cow come and its calf leap.

He shared the milk and found a meal.

Surely, he was happy about the deal,

He awoke and it was only a dream.

Bye and bye comes a cow to give a meal
To her little one she loved so dear.
He was not dreaming now, it was real;
He moaned for one to come by near.

He asked, "Is there no one to care,
To lend mercy and love to share?
Surely, there must be one to dare
My hunger and my burdens to bear.

If true for a calf, how much more
For a poor human should be in store!
But the rich does not open his eyes nor
See the hungry cross to the other shore.

He had on him a small piece of rag
And a small stick he did have to drag.
Had nothing but poverty if any to brag
Seemed it was time his grave to be dug.

In a distance he saw a lady that day,

And hoped she would come his way,

For he had something to her to say,

To give him food or dying down he lay.

Certainly she did come to pass bye;

Oh, how her heart was moved with sigh!

As she came closer and looked at his eye;

She could not go on and let him there to die.

Days without food he was skin and bone;

He can hardly stand up and walk along.

Kind she was and took him to her home

Adopt him for a son never more to roam.

It seemed he was like many given to doom.

In his early days knew nothing but gloom;

She brought him in and took him to a room.

With this experience his life began to bloom.

Tragic! Some have enough to throw,
While others to the garbage they go
To find food to eat, but oh, no,
Riches and poverty what a law!

She did not hesitate to figure out or to even blink.
Quickly she gave him food to eat and milk to drink.
Soon his soul recovered from death's awful brink.
This act of kindness made him cry, weep and think.

As he sat there he remembered his mother
Who died leaving him and his only brother.
His brother died soon after of high fever, too.
He lost all, even his father, in a year or two.

In kindness she said,
"I know how you feel I myself was once there;
Whatever I have shall all be yours to as my heir.
If you don't mind I would take you for a son
Till we die and our journey on earth is done."

Time was given to humanity full of woe.

Sooner or later everyone will have to go,

It was decreed by the Almighty long ago;

There will be an end for poverty man's foe.

All that we have if we can truly share,

What bliss 'twill be son to be my heir!

Many a man has been lost, lost out there

Forgetting his neighbor and didn't care.

We do not want our eyes to close as though blind

Like Dives the rich man, who didn't care or mind.

For the unfortunate like Lazarus covered with sore,

We have a mandate from our Lord and cannot ignore.

Yes, we have to provide for ourselves, if we could,

The things we need – shelter, clothing, and food.

Necessities we cannot do without, and not so free;

Everybody has to work, it is an awesome decree.

However, there are those that are less fortunate,

Must not be forgotten until it is way too late.

No food, clothing and shelter, it is a grim fate.

Don't pass them by like Dives, sitting at your gate.

There lived another man, who kept the law.

Once he ran to the Nazarene and bowed low.

Asked the Master of something he wasn't sure,

What he must do heaven's splendor to secure.

He did not want his destination to look

Like that of many he read in the Book.

He asked if there was anything to help flee,

The woeful dread of death and set him free.

A learned man of the law was he a great teacher.

"What shall I do to enter life? Please tell me Master."

Eagerly he listened the Master give the answer,

Thought there was no lack for something better.

He was not only a versed man but also rich,

Nor did he give time for laughter not an inch.

With all diligence and positive attitude of mind

He set forth to seek happiness, a treasure to find.

The Master answered,

Good, but one thing you still need.

To be complete in the sight of God,

Sow the seed of kindness and of love.

Sell out and give it all, a golden deed,

Clothe the poor and the hungry feed.

Take up thy cross and follow me,

Sacrifice it demands if need be.

You will the crown of life receive

Promised for those who believe.

Young lawyer thought it would be folly

To sell all he owned and to distribute totally.

Grieving he departed, had nothing to say

The price set was too much for him to pay.

Back to the lady kind and full of grace

Who would make our earth a better place.

People need people who are very helpful

To the needy, hungry, ragged and woeful.

It was the month of September so serene

Flowers bloom, with grass, plants, trees green.

They added quite a scene to mountains nearby.

The wheat fields are golden, the stacks are dry.

The rainy season (summer) is almost past

With its scarcity of food to be gone at last.

The harvest time is approaching very fast,

The fatness of the land its shadows forecast.

The village had a small parish school

And the local weather usually was cool.

Lady, now his mother, bought him tools

Ayn` Alem enrolled, 'twas one of the rules.

He was only twelve and not too old

To start school and come to the fold;

To learn a lot and his mind to mold

Gain the knowledge the teachers uphold.

He was first in class, what a surprise,

And received a blue ribbon for a prize.

His mom made him suit one his size

Her face glowed like full moon rise.

He studied hard day and even night,

Devoured his lessons, oh, what a fight!

Every lesson shed a new life and light

In his heart and mind, wonderful sight!

He finished his grade school in years three

Soared high like a bird in the sky flying free.

With nobody to match him in any measure,

Graduation soon came with all its pleasure.

It was a mission school where Christians taught

The Gospel of Christ, salvation by faith wrought.

They had a small chapel where people met to pray.

Ayn `Alem knelt down his guilt on the altar to lay.

You ask me if he were "born again."

He made a decision and it was certain,

To share the good news others to gain

The spring of life an everlasting fountain.

How he ended is left for you to judge.

I wish you like him stand on hedge;

Hear the call and carry on the pledge.

Direct the lost to the cross the only bridge;

To heaven, God's kingdom, man's hope,

A mansion, matchless, beautiful abode

For all the saints as their eternal home.

I would that we like the lady always be

Kind, caring the poor around us to see.

We have only this life and we must share

Blessings graced to us to love and to care.

Obedience without delay

Like Isaiah of old say,

Here am I Lord, send me

Wherever you want me to be.

A young girl he came to love

In the village, a gift from above.

A Christian she was a devout,

The time came to marry no doubt.

Husband and wife they were to share

Their life with all its odds not so fare.

Both began a new wedded life of love

That was at first in the heart of God.

Their mutual love was so profound

That was evident to people around.

The Lord blessed them with children,

Let the mothers say, "Amen!"

Poem two:

The Less Fortunate

There are those in poverty's clutch

Whose dwellings are more like shacks.

They do not have enough, let alone much

Of ragged clothing and half covered backs.

No clean water no bread to live by

The body is weak and the skin dry.

Bones sticking out and sunken eyes

The old moan and the young ones cry.

Mothers weep and the fathers groan
For lack of food their children moan.
The story is true not a fairy tale,
Life is priceless, it isn't for sale.

Many cry for help in such despair
For someone to care, another to share;
To heed their plea and ease their pain
Task so enormous a challenge to dare.

To answer these cries we must rise
Heal their wound and ease the pang.
Raise our banner to hills so high
Faith at work to change their camp.

Clothe the poor and heal the lame
Rescue them and relieve their plight;
Proclaim hope in Jesus' name,
Be of courage and shine your light.

Friends, there's hope it is not the end.

God is still looking he is not done yet

Helping hands to those who are weak.

The answer is in you to heal the sick.

Look to the one who loves to lend

Helping hands our God will send,

Like Isaiah of ancient who truly say,

"Here am I Lord send me, if you may."

Many live in harsh heat and freeze

Bound in chains of poverty in leash,

While the majority relax carefree,

In comfort and watch people perish.

Some cry for water some cry for meat,

Some cry for shelter some cry for heat.

Some cry for help some cry for peace,

Some pray to God some wait for wheat.

Don't travel far to cover ground
The less fortunate are all around.
Open your heart, fill with empathy
Walk a block to discover poverty.

If you really desire to lift the burden
Of the weary and of the heavy laden,
Possibility, destination to change,
Rests in you to take the challenge.

They may not in kind pay you back
Help them 'cause you know their lack.
Throw your bread into the deep water
You will reap harvest sooner or later.

Kindness, goodness be your guide
They will sustain you in the fight.
It is difficult task to do what's right
Gird up and toil till you see the light.

Blessings come from heaven above

For those who give whatever they have.

To lead the poor from misery route

The Master calls to those who would.

Answer the call harvest to gain

Sow kindness undo their chain.

To heal those afflicted in pain

You've the power, don't disdain.

Attempt not alone to tackle the task

Call others to join you, fear not to ask.

Need is vast, you have to recognize

Working together you must organize.

A cup of water to the less fortunate

Fear not to provide whatever it may.

When the books open on that great day

It will be noticed if given in His name.

Not the size of the amount you invest,

It is your intention that God will bless.

If you sell out for the kingdom's sake,

Remember to invest in the unfortunate.

May God help you to hear the cry

Of the unfortunate who live nearby.

Love one another and share the grace

Accumulate treasure in heavenly place. Amen!

Poem three:

Village Life in Zobar

Zobar, a landscape of rarer sketch

Where the sun shines and rivers maze,

Mountains rise and valleys stretch

Clean streams flow and animals graze.

Over the hills cotton-like clouds loom
Against the blue sky a pleasant bloom.
Physical features breath taking vista
It is rural life suitable for quiet fiesta.

In villages spread across the land
Farmers and nomads live in clans.
They have plenty of leisure time
To chat and share ancestors' might.

Some perch on mountain slopes
Where the air is cool and wind blows.
Others spread in gorgeous valley low
Where corn, wheat and barley grow.

Most families live in small homes
Some flat roofs and others of cones.
Size of dwelling won't be an issue
Love for the clan is everyone's due.

Nothing impressive, design of old

Built to protect from heat and cold;

A few feet high, a few yards across

For them a need, for others is a loss.

Animals are parts and parcel of life

Need shelter and protection alike.

The needy ones share the inner fold;

The rest stay within fenced threshold.

Family members work out in the field;

During a long day under a scorching sun

Tree shades provide cool spots for shield,

The gentle wind works like a cooling fan.

Family gets home just before sundown

Yet still have some chores to be done.

Check on the animals if all are in and safe,

Milk the cows and goats and provide hay.

The mother hurries to prepare food
Barley flour bread and lentil soup;
Calls the girls to give her a hand,
Fix the meal for the hungry gang.

Around a small fire children are sitting,
The bread is done and the kids can smell.
Everyone is ready and anxiously waiting
Supper is ready and the children can tell.

Bread is mixed with soup in a dish of clay
It was their custom for the father to pray.
Food is ready the father blesses the meal
After a long day it is time to eat for real.

It is soaked in butter and spicy hot
Don't ask why for it is real shot.
It calls for more if you like it or not;
This is the way it was, it is their lot.

There are no facilities like nowadays.

Firewood for heat and wood fire for light,

The moon and stars to guide their ways

Is all they have for dark and lonely night.

To help them see things near by

To milk the goats, to milk the cow,

To boil the milk and cook some fry

A small candle is all they ask for now.

They have no wealth of great value;

Love for the clan is their treasure true.

A treasure of great price it is their moor,

They share their joys and sorrows tour.

Their distinctive love for one another

Lends a hand the family to stay together;

Marriage covenant of father and mother

Provides anchor to make life smoother.

When the saints heard the call of the Lord,
They crossed mountain tops and vast plains.
They traveled far and preached the Word.
Clans received the Gospel and Christ's reign.

Simplicity of clan life is truly clear;
In its own way it is unique not a leer
To see people sitting in group to hear
One telling a story or rehearse a dream.

What a wonder, who would even think,
To venture places the Gospel to bring
To tribes so far away from civilization
To proclaim God's love and redemption!

They are on the move from here to glory
To meet loved ones who've gone before.
Sailing the skies and shouting victory,
Enter heaven and rejoice for ever more.

They invite us today to join them aboard

The old ship of Zion heaven ward bound.

Christ Jesus Captain of the vessel on board,

They won their battles and lost no ground.

Forward we march like them of old;

We'll face the enemy that is our draw.

Countless difficulties, sacrifices untold

Ready to stand for the truth we know.

Poem four:

I Miss My Mom

A few years was I when she passed away
Old enough just to remember her face;
And a few words of love that stayed
Through the years like stone engrave.

A mother she was gentle, full of grace,
Her life was short but what a short race.
Passionate, caring and full of love
She was a beauty like no other one.

The more I thought of her day or night,
Loneliness gripped my soul from within.
The way grew dark and I saw no light
It didn't go away, it was my escort.

Now, something different I feel,

My body growing, I can see;

Some changes suddenly peal

Changes that are subtle to me.

An inner struggle within, conflict began

Must be resolved and cannot be shunned.

I searched for answers for my poor soul,

For some solace and much needed console.

I sought for some comfort from my peers

Peers I don't really admire nor were cool.

Where can I go but to those that are near

Find answers for my pains to soothe?

I needed her more than ever, my delight

Share my restless and lonely nights.

For a friend, a friend to talk to and cry,

My soul's yearning to cheer and lullaby.

Lying in bed tossed from side to side

The nights are long and sleep is gone;

Tears in my eyes, my eyes open wide

Oh, how I yearned to talk to my Mom!

My father remarried, I guess it was okay;

As for me I would have preferred that not.

For reasons unknown, I couldn't, if I may,

Replace the mom I lost when six, what a lot!

I began to look at things around scroll

And my world grew weird all the more;

A fierce brute, fear gripped my soul,

Fear I have never, never known before.

It felt like all eyes staring at me, a waylay;

Had no clue why I was overly conscious.

I couldn't hide my fear, it won't go away;

It is me, the same girl, changes not so obvious.

The once jolly girl has now no clue

Boys and girls appear different, too.

She is suspicious of people nearby.

Nobody would tell her the reason why.

Mom's face flashes in dreams at night,

My mind is crowded and body aching sore.

My soul dying within me, losing a fight,

I couldn't keep up with school anymore.

As dreadful nights to endless days gave way,

I found no confidant to pour my soul's sigh;

But hid my struggles within for many a day,

Only to learn it worsened as time went by.

My soul was about to give up within me

The burden crushing, leaving its mark;

My mind a bit confused, couldn't see,

Once a happy girl is now left in the dark.

Had a sister three years younger than I
Who confided in me her secrets to share
Need not carry burdens like that of mine;
She can place her trust, she knew I care.

Since I was a few years older than her,
She had me as a source of help somewhat.
For such a time as this one needs a sister
To talk heart to heart as friends one on one.

Nature has its own timing and never amiss
The daughters of Eve reach a certain age.
It is the mystery of nature's law to operate
To fill earth with humans after God's image.

There are numberless young ones held at bay
Who miss their moms as I did mine for long.
Many carry their pain within and always pray
Try to hide their struggle as if nothing wrong.

I missed my mom for things untold

Her sweet voice and her big smiles;

The good breakfast when morning cold,

And evening chat around the wood fires.

Never missed her as I do now,

I don't understand why and how.

I miss my mom, my soul's sad cry,

If I had eagle's wings so I can fly

And bring her back from the sky.

But I don't know the place, a city far away,

Yonder over where the stars are in blaze.

Someday I will get there and be able to say,

"I Missed you, Mom." 'Twill be a joyful day.

Poem five:

Think of **Possibilities**

Son of man, what do you see?

A valley of dry bones!

Can these live again?

You alone know, Lord!

Was the prophet's reply.

I was not to write this

Got carried too far.

You were in my heart

It is an opportunity

I cannot let to waste.

I hope you don't mind

If I digress from my duty.

It is a privilege to speak

Heart to heart as we all need.

There is nothing wrong

For the elders to give advice

To their young ones and

Share experiences of great price.

The youth will need it,

Don't minimize.

It is gold refined by fire

Life lessons that lend to the wise.

Warn the youth of the danger

The world has out there,

Waylaying like a dangerous beast

To ensnare them like little fowls.

Too many alarms – do wear them down.

Rob their vigilance – dull their mind.

Snatch them unaware – lure their heart.

Pull them into the quagmire –

where they cannot come out.

Son of man do your part,

Throw out the life line

Help them catch on.

You will be happy

You rescued a dying soul.

It is human to err we know.

Sometimes we fall face down,

It hurts quite a bit

And a little nose bleed.

We don't have to stay down;

It won't help to give up trying.

Those who succeed

Seven times fall.

For failure is

Head or Tail of life's icon.

We are not perfected yet,

Everyone has his own pot holes.

Flat tires are inevitable,

We all need some spare insoles.

Young people take heed

Pot holes are everywhere.

Those can inflict damage

Watch, adjust, steer your wheel.

Listen to the wisdom of the elders:

Hear, listen, perceive and understand.

They are invaluable resources

Money cannot buy.

Wisdom calls from its towers

With voices loud and clear,

"Come, embrace me as your kin,

Drink of me the water of life,

You will need me in life's desert land."

Don't fool yourself, seek wisdom.

In understanding lies your gain.

Those who despise wisdom

Deprive themselves of treasures.

There are many things we like to have

This side of earthly life.

At the top of the long list

I would say is companionship.

It wasn't good for man to live alone

Was the truth told in the Garden.

The animals were male and female,
Adam was lonely, I can imagine.

The Lord God knew it won't be good
For Adam to live by himself.
He put him to sleep
So he can take from his side.

Eve was perfectly made
A female for male to be,
Presented by God the first bride
That caused Adam's heart to smile.

Beauty is in the eyes of the beholder,
That inner beauty nobody can tell
From outside until one comes near
Face to face with that beautiful thing.

I was once a young lad
Didn't know what it meant
Until I fell in love
With a beautiful one.

She captured my heart
Like a wild young hart.

There were others
More beautiful it seemed
From the outside.
I am glad I didn't fall for that.

I would have regretted
knowing where they are now.
It is good to listen
To the quiet voice
That whispers into your heart.
When everything is hushed
You can hear the pin fall.
There is that quiet voice
Though nobody can hear
What it was
Except the one
On whose ears it fell.

I am ringing the bell

Because it is my duty

To tell everyone

How I feel about it.

If I don't — I will be guilty

Of crime, a foul felony.

This is my message and my role

I wouldn't hide it within my soul.

I am not tired to say it again

My children's attention to gain.

The possibilities are there

For us to discover,

The sky is the limit

To what can be conquered.

Who beguiled you to look down,

Negative thoughts to entertain?

Don't say, "I just can't."

Destination is in your hands.

Look deep inside you and see

The precious jewel within

There is nothing like it;

It is the most priceless pearl.

You can't go to the market place

And put a price on it.

Behold the beauty that is you,

So intricate, wonderful and marvelous

Work of art you will perceive.

This is from my heart to yours,

I just spelled it out.

You know the gist of it,

Keep going, be on the run,

Yes, it is a lot of fun.

Poem six:

A Challenge

Greetings in the name of the Lord
Best wishes and riches in his Word
To you young ones from God above
And from those on earth below, love.

On chariots with the decor bright
If our wishes, we would have you ride
Under the sun shine at noonday light
Groomsmen in uniform and the bride.

We just had one a few days back,
Hope to have many more to luck.
Who next? Ghenet, Meraf ...okay!
You better get ready for your day.

Days give way to weeks and years fly,

Take heart, tomorrow may not come by.

Do not stand still you may be left behind.

Open your eyes, your heart and your mind.

People have their own lots,

I do not know if this is mine:

A mission to call young ones

To recognize their grape vine.

Harvest time has come, summer is past;

Today is your time to prepare the vats.

Don't wait when your grapes are ripe;

Press the grapes fill your pots with wine.

Reapers are busy working in the day's heat

To gather in the barley and store the wheat.

Busy threshing floors, men pray for no rain,

Until they have gathered in the golden grain.

You are on course to your destination;

Follow the example of past generation.

Take heed it may be rough and winding;

Read the road signs, the signal warning.

Many think they can make it without God;

Forget the wiles of life are nothing but sod.

Don't depend on self, have God on your side.

Trust, he will be your ever present guide.

Don't be consumed by love on first sight,

Need not rush to conclusion, watch the light.

Sometimes it is faint and at times 'tis bright;

Watch if your prospect will shine in the night.

The driver in you had stayed concealed

Like a polar bear in a cold winter retreat.

Once nature's ignition is turned on,

You need good brakes, it is no joke.

Love has its night, morning, and noon,

But this thing sprouts like mushroom,

Overnight after the rain and lightening,

Don't be surprised that is our making.

It is very inviting for the unaware green,

Make sure you know the driver within.

It can be very destructive if not tamed

Like a growling wild cat inside a cage.

You may be young and not yet fully grown,

But you got to learn to walk on your own.

Can't depend on your parents for too long,

Before you know it, they may be gone home.

Learn the skills that you need in life now,

Master the art of independence, don't cow.

Don't be dismayed if you stumble and fall,

If not, you'll be crawling when others walk.

I grew up a shepherd boy, had my share
Two young female calves, another a male,
One white, another striped black on white,
A fourth much older and a mother thrice.

They were my joy though I worked hard
Led them to pastures till the day got dark.
They were taken care of, grew fatling true,
A shepherd's delight, like the morning dew.

It was time to find shepherds that knew
How to take care of them more than I do.
I had to make sure they were in good hands
People who had the skills in cattle ranches.

You are aware of the moral of my insert.
Had two of my own, we had to let glean.
No regret for whatever we had to invest
To prepare them to have life of their dream.

Entrusted them to the ones they like,

Friends cheered as they walked the isle.

White wedding gown, awesome sight,

'T was a moment, emotion at its height.

They are in good hands; I don't worry a bit,

Grain in store — enjoying the fruit: oh, 'tis fit!

It is harvest season—everything mighty fine.

Winepress is busy—-wineries stocking wine.

Our daughters are married, no more waddle,

Have infants of their own to hug and cuddle.

No's and yes's have become custom of grace,

As curious minds crawl from place to place.

Don't be scared, take courage to dare;

It was and still is the Lord's will to care.

Make sure to prepare and in yourself invest;

You will never regret for every penny spent.

Don't slack off, you need to be on track
Pursue your goal till you reach the mark.
It is the best gift you can ever find in life
True companion, gold refined by fire.

Young men gawk for their counterpart
For one that would capture their heart.
Hopeful young ladies watch the stride
Of those who might brush off their pride.

They are afraid to jump over the blockade,
Get closer and pull off the pretension façade.
Blind dates may not be the way to generate
Conducive environs you would like to create.

Looking across the fence yonder, stop.
What you see closer is better, I agree.
Use microscope and not a telescope
To watch things nearby details to see.

Start the day with honest short prayer
For guidance the right person to meet;
For a companion nature's best to share
Moments you will hold dear and sweet.

Nothing hard, 'tis possible for the Lord
To bring onto your path one you know
That will spark and set your heart aglow.
Your part is to prepare your field and sow.

You never know when it might be
Wish you all that, so I can see
That beautiful day coming for you
When we hear you say, "I do."

Hey, just thought dropping this for you,
It might strike the right chord for a tune.
If it is the right moment, it may be soon.
I hope to stir up some dust on the moon.

Have guts and reality face,

It's alright, don't be afraid.

We were all in time in this case

But parents had won their race.

       We wish you the best. Amen!

Man, What a Creature

Man was created in God's own image.

After his likeness created he them

Male and female placed in a Garden

The most beautiful Garden of Eden

To enjoy creation's beauty then

Fruits, flowers and animals, what a stage!

A beautiful place, God's handiwork, amazing:

Tiger cabs playing and young lambs grazing,

Bunny rabbits hopping and young deer gazing,

Little birds are singing and ducklings bathing.

Man's dominion was established in his cradle.

His Maker granted him the power to rule

Over creatures land and sea, large or small,

But Adam sold his birthright and forfeited all.

In the garden, God planted one particular tree

A Statue of Fidelity, an eternal covenant to be.

'T was the tree of Knowledge of Good and Evil,

An object of temptation sabotaged of the Devil.

Adam was never to eat from its fruit lest he die.

There were plenty fruit trees from which to try.

Satan intended to thwart God's plan in time due,

Came to Eve as a serpent, she didn't have a clue.

To entertain a thought in her mind to take and eat

He succeeded to beguile Mother Eve to desire it.

She gazed for a moment and saw the beauty

A desire that ushered in human mortality.

Mother Eve ate and gave Adam to share;

He took a bite, I am sure he was aware.

The covering departed, they felt the lack;

Innocence was gone, can't claim it back.

God came to visit man in the cool of the day.

He noticed Adam was not in his usual array,

And called him expecting a happy repose.

Adam answered from his hide out in remorse.

He was not playing with Eve hide and seek,

But under bush cover, overtaken with fear.

Man needed clothing, large leaves won't do.

Animal skin was made into coats for two.

In the mind of God it was not an accident;

He knew afore time there will be an incident.

The Lamb was slain before the world began

To bridge the gap between Creator and man.

God in love sought to bring solace to him,

Killed a lamb, a soul for a soul to redeem.

It was God's way to save Adam's children,

A promise to reclaim what was lost in Eden.

Man's race grope in darkness to find their way.

Virtue was lost, wrong or right people can't say.

Planet Earth couldn't bear man's moral decay,

Such decadence must somehow be held at bay.

Adam was told he would die the day he ate,

One sin led to violence, wickedness and hate.

God moved with grief to destroy his creation

To cleanse the earth and remove abomination.

In the eyes of the Lord — Noah found grace

Heard a voice from God an ark to emplace.

The flood was coming he couldn't ignore,

Told men to repent but they won't implore.

Noah and his family were busy on the beat

To complete the ark and gather animal feed.

Everything was in place and time to enter in

The animals came in pairs: clean and unclean.

The Lord closed the doors nobody can sneak in.

Noah was right when he preached against sin.

The heavens let loose and flood gates released.

Fear gripped man when wrath was unleashed.

Earth was submerged, mountains can't be seen.

Terrestrial creatures all gone as never had been.

Everywhere was the smell of death and putrefaction.

It is the wages of sin, of man's moral degeneration.

Noah waited in the ark for the flood to abate.

He made sure it was safe enough to evacuate.

To worship God for his mercy he built an altar,

And God set the rainbow as covenant forever.

God's redemption plan will never be dead.

Eve's seed would crash the serpent's head.

In Noah the earth will its inhabitants regain.

God promised deluge won't destroy it again.

The sun, moon and the stars on their courses comply,
Will not shy to give their light and glitter in the sky.
Summer, fall, winter and spring will be in operation
Until the ushering in of the new Day of Reformation.

The image of God in man was greatly degraded,
Virtues of love, hope, and faith were debased.
Anger, murder, hate and violence took root instead.
For redemption the blood of the Lamb must be shed.

In time God sent his Son, born of a virgin
For offering, unblemished, who knew no sin.
Scourged and ridiculed, affliction so gruesome,
The Lamb of God died on the cross as ransom.

In anguish the Nazarene cried, "It is finished,"
Victory is won — the serpent's head crushed.
"Father, forgive them," he whispered to pray,
God's mercy met justice at Calvary that day.

By the blood of the Lamb was redemption bought
Atonement now avails for man long time sought.
Not of human efforts lest anybody would boast,
'T is God's gift in Christ to save to the uttermost.

He died once on Golgotha's hill,
Adam's children sore to heal.
Mercy and justice made a deal,
Atonement for sin became real.

Adam's birthright was restored in Christ to reign;
Man will rule the Earth in justice and truth again.
The archenemy is defeated and doesn't have a deed;
He will have to give back his rule to Adam's seed.

Spiritual darkness is past for those who believe,
Are no more aliens God's promise to receive.
The privilege of adoption and citizenry of heaven,
Reformation in progress till we reach our haven.

Darkness is long gone, now shines the light,
No more groping in the dark, the path is bright.
In Christ there is hope, faith and love in sight,
God in heaven grant us grace to do the right.

Now we see and hear man soaring high,
Invent devices for fan or ease his sigh.
To provide for self comfort and delights
He is striving to reach for higher heights.

Man has tamed and trained many a brute:
The elephant and the little monkey shrewd,
Wild cats and the lion, king of the beasts,
Fowls of the air and seals of the open seas.

East talks to West like next door crew;
Distance has been conquered, it is true.
Even time hard to grasp and understand,
We have become a family of one brand.

Ancient challenges don't mean much anymore:

The depth of the oceans and earth crust core;

The unknown space and further galaxies, blue,

The mountain heights and grand canyons, too.

Placing a brick at a time upon past knowledge,

It took millenniums for man to reach this stage.

He built upon contributions of ancient sages,

Now he stands to reminisce of former ages.

This torch must pass to generations to come

To give light that would outshine the last one,

Darkness to dispel from man's heart and mind,

To peer into new heights to discover or find.

Advances in technology and biochemistries,

In manufacture and data process,

Advances in education and health care deliveries

Declare of man's scientific progress.

It took great men to see beyond the blue sky
A difficult challenge an endeavor to even try.
To launch a machine to land man on the moon,
Who would have thought of it to happen so soon?

It took a few score years for it to be real,
Historical fact, people can't deny, was a thrill;
NASA camp danced for joy and celebration.
Men jumped from their seats with jubilation!

With unspeakable knowledge and great skill
Farther into the galaxies man is peeking still.
Into universe so vast to gain just a glimpse,
He peeps to discover mysteries in the expanse.

It is good to discover and learn from creation
Of principles that set the galaxies in motion.
The Great Mover who sustain every operation,
Learn of the laws, decrees, and regulations.

If man would use knowledge to remove fear,

Despair would give place to hope and cheer;

Bring healing to the ailing sick and weary,

Life to those who know no peace but misery.

With all the knowledge man has on hand

He discovered no drug to cure anger or hate.

He builds destructive arsenal of war heads

Ready for use his kindred to annihilate.

Untold human ravages we witnessed,

War giving rise to another like a seed.

Man at war with himself and his kind,

Lessons of the past are still in our mind.

National interests set the rules of the game.

One's gain is another man's loss and shame.

Round table talks yield no trust nor requite.

Indebted nations have to pay back, no respite.

The poor can't go to courts of appeal.

We can't lie to ourselves, let's be real.

Peace talks put only stitches on cuts.

Stand to guard the truth, let's have guts.

We read in the books of the prophets of old

Man can't pull himself out of the quagmire.

He must return to his Maker, thus we are told,

Before destroying himself by his own bone fire.

Man can only speak of, but can't guaranty

Faith, hope and charity: glues of society.

Sublime virtues man must seek and pursue

Intrinsic values of our humanity to ensue.

The Prince of Peace shall surely come

And man with man shall live in love.

The poor and the rich be alike as one,

Justice shall prevail, justice from above.

The King of kings shall come for sure

Restore to Adam his birthright to rule.

The earth — everything on land and sea,

Ransom paid when he died on the tree.

For freedom Christ has set us free. Amen!!

Poem eight:

Freedom in Christ

It is a matter of fact, we all need friends
To pull us out of the valley of dead ends.
We are all human; everybody has a share
The difficulties of life, burdens we bear.

Problems lie within, you can't deny;
It is nature we could not undermine.
Where love, joy and peace should reside,
Curse, anger and hate do growl inside.

Body of death you carry can't undo;
It sticks as wood to wood with glue.
When you desire to do good, evil sneaks,
Tension develops blood pressure peaks.

It is a condition education cannot alter,

A predicament to bear as it were cadaver.

Guilty conscience accusing for one's wrong,

NY's resolutions won't shape a moral code.

Man missed his calling and had a bad fall

Only God can soothe the bruises of the soul.

He imparted the spirit and he should know

How to heal the wound and give life to all.

Man can't lift up himself from the quagmire,

It is God's grace, something man can't acquire.

It takes God Almighty to show man the way,

To welcome his creature to his celestial stay.

If you accepted Christ as your Savior and Lord,

Don't hide it under bushel, let other people know.

We read in the Holy Scriptures, God's Word,

To let our light shine in darkness and let it glow.

Just in case you meet some feeble soul,
Give a helping hand, it is your divine call.
It is your privilege, don't let them down,
Strengthen the weak till their day dawn.

Those who turn many to the Kingdom
Shall shine like stars in their eternal home.
Crying and sorrow shall never more be,
For freedom Christ has set them free.

There's a highway, the Northeast Main
Directions are clear and no u-turn lane.
Don't turn back, life of sin you must hate,
Keep pressing till you see the pearly gate.

Nothing dangerous there shall in ambush lay.
Travel is safe for all on Moses Expressway.
It is the Way of Holiness, everything clean.
The scenery is beautiful and landscape green.

In the last day when the trumpet sound,
The dead shall rise, take off the ground.
Saints appear before the judgment seat
Clad in white their Redeemer to meet.

Can you see the myriads of saints
Marching through the pearly gate;
Waving palms of celebratory victory
Shouting, "Honor, majesty, and glory?"

From nations, tongues and every tribe,
Washed in the blood their garments white.
They fought the good fight, kept the faith,
Finished their race at the Hallelujah Gate.

In the air there will be joyful fling
It is the marriage supper of our King.
Welcome home his church, his bride
From the first martyr to the ones alive.

Time for holy dance it will surely be
The saints of God have been set free.
"Hallelujah Chorus" everybody sing,
And heavenly bells chime and ring.

No more sorrow and no more sighing
No more death and no more crying;
No more hunger, no more thirsting
No more sickness, no more groaning.

The redeemed of the Lord shall praise
The Redeemer, the Lamb that was slain,
To call all men come back home again
Adam's dominion on earth to reclaim.

Christ, the Messiah shall be the King;
All nations shall their homage bring.
Restoration of creation shall ever be,
For freedom Christ has set us free. Amen!

Poem nine:

On Your Wedding

It is our pleasure to congratulate,
Dear Shanon has found her mate.
It is not easy to find one of a kind,
You are a priceless jewel to find.

We can notice he is gentle and kind
As he walked his mom down the isle.
We saw how he hugged his Mom,
His love was obvious, not a sham.

That will be his character true
It won't change, 'tis honey dew.
Sound of music filled the sanctuary
Lend beauty to the whole ceremony.

Music was rich beyond measure
Keep the record, 'tis a treasure.
Souls were lifted up by the music
Drawn to God like the mystics.

With sparkling eyes and your smile
You were beautiful like a true shrine.
The clock had ticked its final dial
A signal, you can't forget for life.

We are happy and wish you fly
To higher heights to the blue sky.
It wouldn't be easy, I do know,
To jump hurdles high and low.

Keep going you are in the race
God will give you sufficient grace.
Don't depend on your knowledge
Trust God, as you take the pledge.

Your sun is shining in the sky so blue,

June 26, 2010 is here, you'll say, "I do."

Have God always walk by your side,

He will be your true friend and Guide.

"To God be the glory" forever more,

Keep it in your heart as never before.

Life may not be milk and honey flow

But God will give you grace to glow.

Let your love be your holding glue

Not wood to wood but **Joe *and YOU***.

If God bless you with children soon,

They'll be your joy and your boon.

May our God richly bless you two,

And fill your hearts with gladness, too.

I don't know what else to say,

May God guide you all the way. Amen!

In love,

Baba Araia

Poem ten:

On Your Graduation

That little baby I watched to grow
What to make of it is hard to know.
Won't be a dream but we would see
The little girl would someday be.

An MD was too far for me, I confess,
She proved me wrong nevertheless.
I am proud of her genuine progress
Honored to be her uncle, I'm blessed.

My Niece is one of a kind
I can't deny it in my mind!
She is beautiful and so smart
Graceful like the wild hart.

She aspired to higher heights
Glued to chairs countless nights.
Made many a book her best friend
To digest knowledge the sages lend.

To reach her anticipated goal
Winter, spring, summer and fall
Took no breaks through them all
To be there when the roll is called.

The moment came orchestra to play
Graduates in queue without delay,
Friends watched as elites march
Take their place beneath the arch.

My Niece was there among the group
Anxiously waiting to wear their hood.
With cap and gown all dress in black
Crowd was loud wishing them luck.

Sister Love and Uncle Write did well
You are blessed, more than words can tell.
Money can't buy your precious Jewel,
Lahia, God's gift, a priceless PEARL.

Aren't you proud of her as sweet as she
Studious young lady she grew up to be?
Beautiful, gentle, one among the elite,
Unique celebration let the candles lit.

At this moment, Uncle Write is glad
For investing on his daughter's plan.
Sister Love is so elated, that we know
To see her baby achieve her MD goal.

Eight years of stringent discipline
Is what took Beauty her race to win.
Competitions were many in queue
But SUS of Medicine, what ado!

Studying like driving in first gear,

You made our hearts fill with cheer.

Now you are heading up to the peak

We'll see you take the last step my dear.

Congratulation!

Uncle Araia

Poem eleven:

Happy Anniversary My Dear!!

Happy anniversary is what they say

Because it is the custom of the day.

It was the happiest day in our life

And will be treasured I wouldn't lie.

You'll treasure it more than we do

Deeply personal, specially for you.

Your union wasn't coincidence

It is God's will and Providence.

Some may say it is a matter of chance

But I would never give a wink at that.

The Scripture has told us time and again.

We don't take lightly what God has said.

Those that love God will not ever shame;

Things turn good for believers in his name.

From my heart to yours in honesty

My Dear, happy first anniversary!

You two became one on July 12, 2008

Rough or smooth to stick to the FAITH.

God made a way for you to meet,

He promised to supply all your need.

When blessed with children fleet,

Home will fill with aroma sweet.

Oh Lord, keep them safe all the way

Beneath your wings protected to stay. Amen!

In love,

Your Dad

Poem twelve:

My Happy Girl

Selecting a name was quite a task;

Your kith and kin do understand.

Your name was not a random pick,

Parents have pondered quite a bit.

Such a special name to choose,

I can imagine the time it took.

Tsega or Billie won't really do

For 'Hannah' sweet honeydew.

Favor of God's love to share

Was entrusted to parents to care.

You weren't a matter of chance

But God's plan in you to enhance.

Wonderful and intricate design
Engraved in you is image divine.
It can't be denied, let's be frank;
It is the truth, not a myth or prank.

His likeness in ones like you
Brings joy to his heart, 'tis true.
Your innocence and pure at heart
Was God's intent from the start.

One more soul has come to life
That never was before in time.
Whenever a baby is born alive,
It makes the heart of God smile.

My dear, we shall see you grow
To be a channel for love to flow;
A light house in darkness to shine,
Wayfaring men to see the sign.

It is our sincere desire and prayer
For you to be a significant player.
In the service of the Most High
It is a higher calling, never be shy.

You captured their heart's core;
They can't ask for anything more.
Can't imagine the joy they felt;
You will be their driving belt.

Beautiful work of divine art
You are the joy of the heart:
A hidden pearl, a priceless jewel,
An energizer, a high power fuel.

Parent's life was quick to change
To focus on you at every stage.
There's none like you for them
You'll always be their lovely gem.

Digital cameras often are on stand by
To catch moments before they die:
Precious memories of invaluable price
Family treasure and parents' prize.

Parents do shop for the day's style
Their joy to add goodies to the pile.
Toys, books, shoes are in stock
When done, put them on the rack.

You've everything money can buy
Chest drawers are full, closets pry.
Liberty and bounty are sure to be
In the land where people live free.

Music is your life; in you 'twill stay;
It is your joy nobody can take away.
Always keep your music in sight;
It will bring joy, peace and delight.

I cannot forget your sign language;
You made it look so easy to engage,
And to communicate your message.
You are awesome, it is an advantage.

You are now blessed with twins
Precious gifts, Levi and Benjamin.
They are cute and lovely, real boon;
Watch, they will be running soon.

Be gentle, handle them with care;
Now, three of you have to share.
You are first and always will be
The source of joy and our jubilee.

Levi and Ben are still delicate, too,
But watch them add a pound or two.
They will be trailing you very soon
To the zoo, park, museum and school.

Remember your mom who pays

Sleepless nights and restless days

To provide the best care she knew,

And glad to have done so for you.

I set out to write a few lines

From this small heart of mine

To get you to laugh and smile.

Adios for now, hope 'twill suffice.

Abba Hagoy Araia

Poem thirteen:

Through It All

Through many unspeakable difficulties
In the midst of horrifying hostilities,
Feb 27, 1978 was a monumental day;
No storm, however strong, can delay.

The sky was clear and the sun bright.
The air was quite, no F15 blights.
Some on foot and others on bikes
Joined our group to take our bride.

We were ushered in to take our seat.

The bride in white joined the feast;

A day of celebration the first to be

For the family between her and me.

Feb 27, 1978 was a special date.

Seated on chairs, our elders in sight

Sharing food from the same plate,

It was a happy day, families delight.

Wasn't the first time, but a special one

The consummation of our mutual love.

We were soon to receive warm assent

From family elders who were present.

Finishing lunch and benedictions done,
'T was time to start the trip back to town
Where friends were waited for us to come
To conclude ceremony before sundown.

Celebration was brief, 'tis unfortunate.
We were by distance again to separate:
Bride in Asmara and groom in another
Conflict in between perilous, altogether!

Back to Asmara had to escort my bride,
Taking the risk of being locked inside.
May not let me out, security so tight
A second attempt nearly cost my life.

Life for life man would anything give.
Regional conflict made it hard to live.
Staying in Asmara for her wasn't safe;
Disguising herself was the way to escape.

Security so tense to make one sick,

Our only option was to take a risk.

When we made it through the last post,

We felt the relief, our souls reposed.

We were united again together to stay,

But events soon worsened day by day.

We had no group or political affiliation

That might help assuage our situation.

July 25th 1978 we shall never forget;

War planes made our school a target.

Napalm explosions inflicted demolition;

Visible scars still remain for generation.

Their blasts take one's breath away

While people run for shelter to stay.

Their screeching sound chills the spine,

One holds breath till he hears the strike.

Enemy forces drawing from the south
Was a sad day for us–for them a shout.
Freedom Fighters couldn't hold ground,
"Withdraw!" echoed an alarming sound.

Eritreans never anticipated such dislodge;
It was said the retreat was only a dodge.
For civilians left behind, all hopes crashed,
Bad memory where heart and mind clashed.

She was a defector, could end in jail;
Can't wait in town, had to follow the train.
On July 28, 1978, we left town at twilight
As the Ethiopian army was soon to arrive.

Unable to pick anything we owned
Began our voyage into the unknown.
From a distance, we saw our place choke
Under thick cloud–dark pillars of smoke.

Our hearts gripped with consternation,

Wife: pregnant, anemic, and frail,

On foot, uncertain of our destination,

Bewildered, we began the long trail.

I can't forget the first day away from home,

A heart breaking scene devoid of any hope;

When she lay under a tree to sleep,

A nurse, a bride, pregnant, a stranded sheep.

There are always people, thank God,

Who would share what little they got.

Their character, I say, compassion pure,

For souls in pain grant healing and cure.

Shocking events we had seen a few

Our vehicle stalled and brakes failed.

We were not aware, not even a cue,

Thanks to a man his efforts prevailed.

Now, a second time on a sharp curve
Going downhill, can't complete a turn.
Attempted to reverse, brakes won't hold,
It was nothing short of miracle been told.

If we were into the ravine to plunge,
No soul would have survived the slump.
Had it not been God reaching out to save,
None of us would have been alive today.

I believe in God's saving grace
And will see Him face to face.
I believe in His love,
He gave His only Son
The Passover Lamb.
I believe in the blood
Of the crucified One.

We reached Keren, a strategic town
Delimited by mountains all around,
Last strong hold for a battle ground,
Between forces who want the crown.

Staying with our good friends was a lure,

But the fall of the city was inevitably sure.

We were on a long journey but not a tour;

To reach our destination we had to endure.

Anticipating difficult travel through the wild,

We arranged to hire a guide and camels to ride.

First attempt failed and I was escorted to jail;

Three days and two nights were a nightmare.

My wife didn't know my whereabouts.

Her hope snatched away she can't scout.

She was alone sitting outside the house,

Unkind thought deranging her with doubt.

She was in shock nobody could blame,

Human behavior is all around the same.

In such predicament, any would behave,

It is our nature there is nothing profane.

I was released after paying a sum for fine;

A second attempt could be gray or shine.

Hassle and bustle all around, life on the line,

We had to be quick and cannot waste time.

Our path was lit with full moon light,

We made it safe despite our fright.

We met our guide, everything alright,

And began our seven day journey flight.

Sleeping at night under the starry sky,

We saw our dreams fade and wishes die.

Our pillow a stone, mattress the sand to lie,

Faith our strength, had no reason to decry.

For safety we traveled till late nights,

Crossing valleys and ascending heights;

Partly on foot and partly on camel ride,

Our feet were sore but cannot repine.

It was over two months since we left home,

And my wife had only two months to go.

Seven months pregnant on camel saddle,

You can imagine the risk and the hassle.

Thank God! We crossed the border safe;

We found an old friend, with her to stay.

She provided care money cannot repay.

We recovered fast, ready next step to take.

Destination in mind, Wad el Hilew next:

A refugee camp, political breeding nest

To start life with no money down at best,

Won't be easy but have a place to rest.

We started our trip on top of a lorry

On dirt road, quagmire when rainy,

Stopped over night at a post nowhere,

Mosquito infested, we had our share.

Another day another venture ahead lay

A few hours trip became several days.

We had no food supplies on hand now,

Except from those who are sent of God.

Every situation when lack was for real

It was supplied more than we can dream.

In all that, there was always someone

That would show sympathy and act in love.

Arrived at Wad el Hilew refugee camp,

A village along the Tekeze River bank,

We met friends there and decided to land.

Through it all, we saw God's hand raised

Had a reason to call our first born ***Praise.***

Your eternal hope, you do show

When you let God's love flow;

And in the dark your light glow

Christ in you let the world know.   Amen!

Poem fourteen:

Everything is Alright

It was in Um`gur`gur, a remote village
A UN camp for Eritrean refugees,
A place devoid of modern facilities,
Habitat for scorpions and rattle snakes.

Mom was a nurse — attending the sick.
Mother baby unit — in a Swedish clinic,
She was pregnant — our second child
Painful it will be — it won't be mild.

Count the due date – can't postpone,
Nature has its way — cannot carry on.
Carillon sounded – tot at the door,
The body is on fire – ready to roll.

It was past noon, on January 29, 1980

Contractions were regular with intensity.

Had to see the nurse, a good neighbor

Exam took place and was time for labor.

A nurse, a guard, myself — the three

Crowded in a tiny birthing room to be.

Eve's daughter lay in a small clinic bed;

Bravery is a plus and tolerance is at red.

There was no anesthesia readily available

To make her twinge somewhat tolerable.

"Push on my back!" Lem screeched at me.

Message well taken, wish I can set her free.

I was powerless to help ease her anguish,

Suffering no man on earth can vanquish.

I stood baffled there was nothing I can do,

Heart pounding and pulse throbbing, too.

She might have cringed twice or thrice;
Can't alter nature, it won't do otherwise.
Collected her strength to finish the task,
She pushed the little creature out at last.

Labor was short, nature its blessing lend,
But methinks it was eternity without end.
The baby saluted her attendees with a cry,
"It is a girl!" declared the nurse in reply.

And she whispered, "Call her "Senait!"
Astounding it is, after such grueling pain,
To say, "It is well and it will be alright!"
Amazing how mothers dare to do it again.

Hard to recollect what happened later
Have to ask her if she can remember.
What else took place in that tiny cell
My mind can't recall, no ringing of bell.

Mothers had to go home after delivery,

Because they had no room for recovery.

Mom and baby came back on a jeep

To recover at home, to rest and sleep.

Mosquito infested camp – refugees' goad

Feels it was their only – breeding moat.

Malaria claimed lives – infants in peril

My baby wasn't exempted – such an ordeal.

Our little baby had to fight illnesses

Malaria, fever and related anomalies.

To provide means we were work bound

And keep our two girls safe and sound.

We were blessed to have a good neighbor

Who took good care of us like a mother.

'Twas a relief to find like her in the land

Who understood the case to lend a hand.

Life conditions were harsh and scant,

Don't wish you live in a refugee camp.

It is not where milk and honey flow,

Destitute of comfort, 'tis good to know.

Survival was the key — our driving gear

No handouts there – no wheels to steer.

Hold on to life – don't fall over the cliff

We say a prayer – God to send us relief.

Heat index is high – under scorching sun

No Oasis of Hope – nature its bliss shun.

No gushing water – from Moses' old Rock

To quench thirst – of people and livestock.

Jacob's well had an old diesel motor pump.

Often broke down and took time to fix up.

People waited in line for a tanker to arrive

And get their ration a few gallons at a time.

The day came when we had to say goodbye
To our friends as they wept and stood nearby.
Emotions gripped our hearts, we're uncertain
If we were going to see their faces ever again.

Heading to USA on resettlement program
Was never in our mind nor in our plan.
Arrived in Khartoum, the process took time;
Difficult situation, we had spent every dime.

Hospitality and friendship are joined at the hip;
One can't stand on its own, and expect to leap.
Sharing what one has is not coined as easy loot;
Wasn't a day, 'tis true, we went without food.

While in waiting both got very ill:
 Mother of malaria
 Baby with diarrhea.
Can't lose both, had to choose the lesser evil.

We had to wean her, a situation so difficult,

Cannot lose my fight, her survival is a must.

Giving up wasn't an alternative, 'tis an assail;

Whatever it took I was in for a fight to prevail.

Too young, she cannot yet hard food chew.

She had some teeth and molars just a few.

I had to share mine with her, I'm not a fool;

Desperation drives a parent to break the rule.

With very little intake she made it okay;

My darling endured an ordeal a dire day.

Cow milk in a bottle was ready for use

She is hungry, hoping she won't refuse!

My baby in my bosom as if mom's breast,

She grabbed the bottle, hope for the best.

Emotions overtook my being as a whole;

Words can't express how I felt in my soul.

She took the milk–no more a risk,

Filled her Tommie–no more crick.

Battle was fought – victory wrought,

Beat the odds – let friends shout.

My baby endured,

Won the battle.

Hallelujah!

God is Good! Amen!!

The ORIGINAL
(Happy Anniversary)

The more I think of you

And watched you grow, too

From a baby fragile

To adulthood so mobile.

Your "yea" and "nay" were clear cut;

There was no gray area left for doubt.

When things were wrong

You stood your ground.

You showed compassion to care.

I ask myself, "What a change!"

The real child matured to give

Fruit of love, care and sympathy.

Keep this up for others to see,

God the Father will help you be:

A light in darkness

To lit their path.

I am not flattering

Because you are mine;

From my heart all is fine.

I am just surprised with

What you have become.

Changes: a daughter — a wife — a mother

And more so of your love, care

And concern for others!

Today is your Fourth Anniversary:

A happy one for this and more to come.

God bless you MY DEAR, in love abide

On your anniversary Oct 1, 2009.

Love,

Your Dad

Dr. Araia T. Hadgu is the secretary and active member of Besserat Evangelical Society, a Christian organization that has been providing annual conferences for Eritreans in Diaspora for the last 31 years. He served in this capacity since 1998. He acquired his BA from Kansas City College and Bible School (KCCBS), MA in religious education from Trinity College and Seminary and his PhD in theology from North Carolina School of Theology through correspondence. He is an active member of Besserat Evangelical Church of the Nazarene in Indianapolis, IN. He serves as worship leader and a pianist and assists the pastor.

This is his first attempt to publish a book. Also, *Introduction to Christian Philosophy* in his native language and *My Life's Story* in English are manuscripts he hopes to publish.

CPSIA information can be obtained at www.ICGtesting.com
Printed in the USA
LVOW01s1649181014

409407LV00002B/2/P